To Lydia —N.P.

To every young reader who discovers that
the pen is mightier than the sword—W.M.

Winter Hill

WINNISIMMET

Prospect Hill

Mystic River

Cobble Hill

Phipps Farm

Lechmere
Point

CHARLESTOWN

NOODLES
ISLAND

← Cambridge

Charles River

Mill Pond

BOSTON

Common

South
Battery

Boston
Neck

Dorchester
Hill

BOSTON
ITS ENVIRONS
and HARBOR
1775

ROXBURY

DORCHESTER HEIGHTS

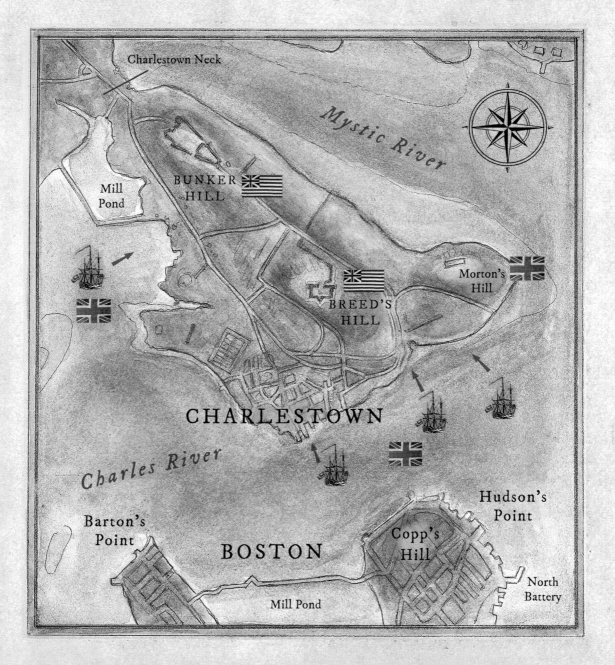

Battle of Breed's Hill and Bunker Hill
June 17, 1775

I. Ben's Boston

In the fall of 1773, the town of Boston was about to change forever. But for twelve-year-old Benjamin Russell, each day passed just like the one before it. His family owned a cow, and in the evening after school, once the cow had been milked in the yard behind their house, he led her back through the crooked streets to the Boston Common. As his cow began to graze on the thick grass of the common, Ben liked to watch the sun set over the cove of salt water called the Back Bay.

Ben also enjoyed helping one of his father's friends, the printer Isaiah Thomas. On a bench at Mr. Thomas's shop were hundreds of tiny metal letters, and Ben loved to fit the letters together into words. He went to school like the other boys in town, but it was at Mr. Thomas's printing shop that Ben learned the power of these otherwise ordinary words. Once they were blackened with ink and pressed against sheets of paper, the words did something altogether wonderful and strange. They told stories that were read by people not only in Boston and Massachusetts but throughout all thirteen American colonies.

II. The Patriots Rebel!

That fall, many of the stories in Mr. Thomas's newspaper, the *Massachusetts Spy*, were about the troubles between Great Britain and her colonies. Great Britain needed money to help pay for the defense of the colonies, and one of the ways of getting that money was to make the colonists pay a tax on tea.

The colonists loved their tea, but many of them, who called themselves "patriots," did not like the tax. More than a hundred years before, their ancestors had come to America so that they could worship as they pleased. The colonists were used to doing things their own way. No one, not even the British government, was going to make them pay a tax on tea. When in December three ships filled with chests of British tea arrived at Griffin's Wharf in Boston, the patriots decided to act.

Smearing their faces with ashes and wrapping themselves in blankets, about 150 patriots disguised themselves as Mohawk Indians. Once aboard the ships, they broke open the wooden chests with their hatchets and dumped the tea into the harbor. As Ben watched the brown tea leaves float away on the tide, someone shouted out, "Boston Harbor is a teapot tonight!"

None of them would ever forget that night, and they called it the Boston Tea Party.

III. Liberty or Death!

For the boys, it was all great fun, but three thousand miles away in Great Britain, no one was laughing. In May of 1774, six months after the Tea Party, a ship arrived in Boston Harbor with a new governor for Massachusetts: Thomas Gage, a general in the British army, who was soon followed by hundreds of British soldiers. It was his job, Gage announced, to close the port of Boston. Until the colonists agreed to pay for the tea they'd destroyed, no more ships would be allowed to enter or leave Boston Harbor.

If the ships couldn't come and go, the Bostonians would be cut off from doing business and wouldn't be able to feed their families. Isaiah Thomas was so angry that he added a headline to the front page of his newspaper that read, "Americans! Liberty or Death! JOIN OR DIE!" All over Boston, people had to make a decision: Were they to do as Isaiah Thomas said and join the patriots, or were they to do as General Gage said and remain loyal to the king?

IV. Go Home, Redcoats!

By the summer, the wharves of Boston were quiet. But the Boston Common was noisier than it had ever been. Instead of mooing cows, the common was full of British soldiers who marched up and down the grassy meadow in their red uniforms to the shrill music of the fife and drum. Sometimes fights broke out in the streets between the townspeople and the soldiers. It was a scary time. Ben and his friends would watch the soldiers from the tree-lined edge of the common. "Go home, you redcoats!" they shouted.

One day in August, Ben learned that a man from Connecticut was approaching the town gate with a gift for the citizens of Boston. His name was Israel Putnam. He had a wide and friendly face and a big stomach, and crowded into his wagon were 130 sheep to help feed the town. Israel Putnam made his way to the Boston Common, where he struck up a conversation with the British soldiers. Fifteen years before, he had fought alongside these same men during the French and Indian War, and he considered many to be his friends. But he had a warning now. "The next time I come to Boston," he said, "I will be your enemy."

V. Boys' Rights

That January, a storm blew in from the north and blanketed Boston in snow. When classes were over at the Queen Street Writing School, Ben and his friends got their wooden sleds to go "coasting" down the icy streets of Beacon Hill.

They started near the mansion owned by the merchant and patriot leader John Hancock, pushing their sleds across the rutted snow and ice until they seemed to be flying down the hill. Ben was leading the pack as they rushed down School Street when suddenly his sled slowed down. Ben was outraged to discover that ashes had been spread across the snow and ice, to make the street less slippery, by the British officer who had moved into a nearby house.

With several friends at his side, Ben marched up the steps of the British officer's house and rapped on the door. The officer was soon at the doorway. Ben explained that for years this was the boys' favorite "coasting" place, and now it was ruined.

To Ben's surprise, the officer ordered his servant to pour water over the ashes. Soon the water had frozen to ice, and they were coasting once again. Ben had been taught to believe that the soldiers were in Boston to take away his liberties. But this officer had proven to be an understanding man.

Later that night, the British officer told General Gage about his encounter with Ben and his friends. The general gave a weary sigh. "No wonder we are having so much trouble with these Bostonians," he said. "Even the children insist on their rights!"

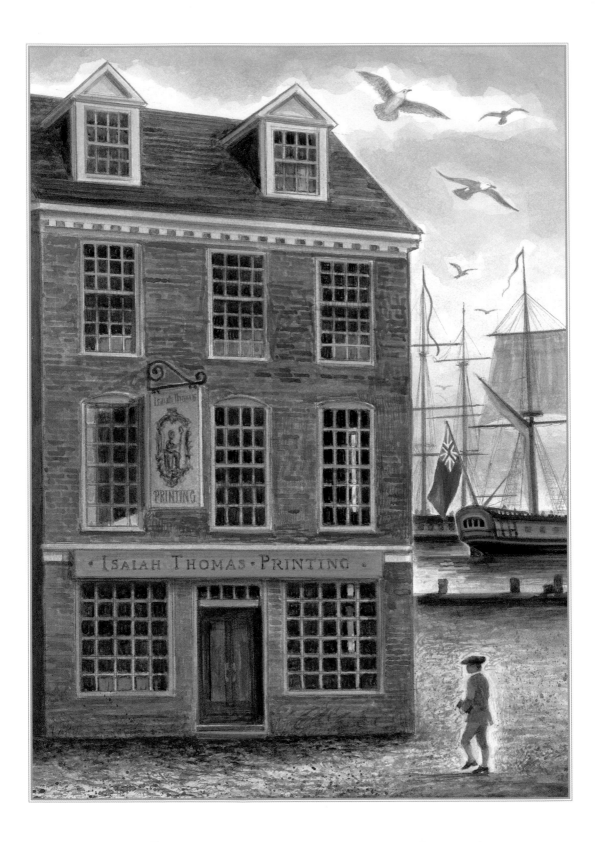

VI. Leaving Boston

In early April, word reached Boston that even more British soldiers were coming and that General Gage was about to start arresting patriot leaders like John Hancock. Fearing that a war was about to break out, many Bostonians decided that it was time to leave. The streets of Boston began to fill with people and their wagons trying to escape across the thin neck of land that connected Boston to Roxbury and the towns beyond.

One day after school, Ben stopped by Isaiah Thomas's printing shop. Usually he heard the *thump-thump-thump* and *clickety-clack* of the printing press even before he opened the door. But this time everything was quiet, and when he tried to open the door, it was locked. He looked through the window and saw that the shop was empty! There was not even a note to say where Isaiah and his family had gone. Up until now, Isaiah Thomas had shown no fear of the British authorities. But if *he* had decided to leave Boston, bad things must be about to happen.

VII. The First Shots!

On the morning of April 19, 1775, Ben walked to the Queen Street Writing School just as he did every day. He and his friends were sitting at their desks when they heard the sound of a fife and drum on the street outside the school. Master James Carter sent a boy out to find out what was happening. He came back with amazing news.

The previous night, General Gage had sent 500 British soldiers on a secret mission to seize the cannons that the patriots had hidden in Concord, about twenty miles away. But the mission had not remained a secret for long. By midnight, patriot riders like Paul Revere and William Dawes were headed out of Boston to alert the countryside that British soldiers were coming.

Each town in Massachusetts had its own militia made up of patriots who were willing to fight for their families, farms, and freedom. When the alarm was spread, thousands of them said good-bye to their wives and children, took up their muskets and powder horns, and headed to Concord. But would the militiamen have the courage to stand up to the British soldiers?

At daybreak on the town green in Lexington, the patriots showed they had the courage. When the British soldiers charged toward them, the militiamen held their ground. The British fired their muskets, and eight militiamen were killed.

When Ben and his schoolmates heard this, they were stunned. After more than a year of mounting tension, people—ordinary people just like them—had been shot dead by British soldiers! It now seemed as if all hopes of settling matters peacefully with the British were gone.

Master Carter looked at them with a solemn yet excited expression on his face. "Boys," he said. "The war's begun, and you may run."

VIII. Yankee Doodle

As soon as the boys got outside, they discovered more than a thousand British soldiers along the length of Tremont Street.

General Gage had been shocked by how quickly the patriots had assembled in the countryside and realized that he needed to send out reinforcements from Boston to aid the soldiers he'd already sent to Concord. There on Tremont Street was General Hugh Percy on his white horse, surprisingly young and elegantly dressed in his scarlet-red British officer's uniform. When the long line of soldiers began to march toward the town gate, Ben called out to his friends, "Come on, let's go!"

It was a beautiful spring day as they followed the soldiers across the neck that led out of Boston. By the time they'd left the city behind and mounted the hill that led to the Roxbury town green, the British fifers had started to play "Yankee Doodle," a song that poked fun at the New Englanders for being silly and rude:

Yankee Doodle went to town,

Riding on a pony;

He stuck a feather in his hat

And called it macaroni.

Benjamin decided it was time to poke fun at the British. As the soldiers sang the words to "Yankee Doodle," Ben began to dance and jump around.

The general looked down from his white horse and asked, "Why, young man, are you laughing so heartily?"

"Oh," Ben said with a mischievous smile, "I'm just thinking of how our militiamen will make your soldiers dance to this tune by nightfall!"

IX. Trapped!

Ben and his friends followed General Percy's brigade across the bridge to Cambridge, on the other side of the Charles River. The boys had grown tired of walking, so they lay down on the grass of the town green and watched the lines of British soldiers continue along the road toward Concord.

After a few hours of lounging in the sun and playing games, the boys began to hear the occasional boom of a cannon. Then they saw the British soldiers marching back from Concord, returning to Boston. They could see General Percy on his big white horse, shouting orders to his men, as patriot militiamen fired on them from behind trees and stone walls. As Ben had predicted, the militiamen had General Percy and his army on the run.

Night was coming on, and in the growing darkness, the boys could see the bright muzzle flashes of the guns. They could also hear a strange whistling sound—almost like the high-pitched buzzing of bees. A militiaman, his face blackened by smoke and dirt, shouted at them with a crooked grin.

"Boys," he called out. "That whistling you hear? That's the sound of musket balls! You'd better get yourselves to somewhere safe quick!"

Exhausted and more than a little frightened, the boys found safety in one of the buildings that belonged to Harvard College in Cambridge, and they spent the night sleeping on the floor. The next morning, they learned that the British soldiers had sealed off Boston to prevent the militiamen from entering the city.

Only then did Ben realize the fix they were in. A war had broken out, and they had no way to reach their families in Boston. They were on their own.

X. A Job for Ben

In Boston, the British soldiers and all the remaining towns-people—including Benjamin's parents—were surrounded by the patriots and cut off from the neighboring countryside. Ben and his friends could only hope that their families would somehow get enough to eat.

Meanwhile, militiamen from all over New England were being organized into what they called the provincial army under General Artemas Ward. General Ward had the difficult job of turning these farmers into soldiers. He also had to figure out a way to feed them all. He needed people known as clerks to count the soldiers and deliver the food. Since it didn't involve fighting, this was the perfect job for Ben and his friends, and they were all eager to make themselves useful.

Ben became the clerk for Israel Putnam, the same chubby, bighearted man from Connecticut who had brought the sheep to Boston the summer before. Israel Putnam wasn't like most of the officers in the provincial army. He didn't wear fancy clothes, and he liked to work alongside his men and joke with them. The boys

called Israel Putnam "Old Put," and every morning, Ben lugged a basket full of provisions out to where Old Put's men were stationed. By early June, Put's soldiers were on a hillside overlooking Boston, where they worked with picks and shovels digging trenches and putting up walls in preparation for the day they knew was coming—the day when the British would march out of Boston and attack.

XI. Defending the Hills

On June 17, 1775, the distant roar of a cannon rocked the streets of Cambridge.

The night before, as Ben lay sleeping, Colonel William Prescott and about a thousand soldiers from Massachusetts and Connecticut had begun digging an earthen fort to defend the Charlestown peninsula against the British. But there was a problem: Colonel Prescott had built his fort on Breed's Hill. The fort was supposed to be on Bunker Hill, a much larger hill a half mile behind Breed's Hill. By building the fort where the enemy could clearly see them, Colonel Prescott had given the British no choice but to attack. He had started what would be one of the bloodiest battles of the Revolution, and no one in Cambridge was ready for it.

Ben and his friends gathered outside the house in Cambridge that was the headquarters of the provincial commander, General Ward. They could hear men shouting and arguing inside, and then suddenly, the front door flew open and messengers started running out in every direction with orders to deliver. Soon regiments of soldiers were hastily assembling on the green and marching off toward Charlestown to help Colonel Prescott.

Having been Old Put's clerk, Ben knew that the highest point in Cambridge was Prospect Hill, where there was a spectacular view of Charlestown and, beyond that, Boston. "Come on," he shouted to his friends. "Follow me!"

XII. Attacked

Once they'd reached the top of Prospect Hill, Ben and his friends could not believe what they saw! British warships were everywhere, firing on the provincial fort on Breed's Hill and on the militiamen streaming across the narrow Charlestown Neck to join the fighting.

The boys could see William Prescott standing atop his fort, waving his sword and yelling at the British as cannonballs sailed through the air and smashed into the dirt all around him. To Prescott's left, hundreds of soldiers were frantically building a barricade that was half stone wall and half rail fence.

They could also see Israel Putnam, one of the few men on a horse, riding back and forth across Charlestown Neck, urging the men to hurry. Every time he came close to Ben and the boys up on their hill, they would jump up and down and cry out, "Huzzah, Old Put!"

XIII. Watching the War

And there, on the other side of the harbor, was the city of Boston. From their vantage point, Ben and his friends could see a fleet of boats assembling on the waterfront near Boston. Hundreds of curious colonists had turned out, dotting the hillsides and crowding the roofs of their houses to watch the battle unfold.

He was too far away to tell, but Ben couldn't help but wonder whether his parents were on one of those roofs, looking for *him*.

XIV. Outnumbered

As the boats approached, Ben could see that each one was crowded with British soldiers, their silver bayonets glinting in the sun.

Once the British soldiers had been rowed across the harbor to the Charlestown shore, they assembled in a long line that extended almost all the way across the peninsula. At their head was General William Howe, a tall man with black eyes and dark hair, who was surrounded by his staff of officers.

Suddenly, a British warship fired a different kind of cannonball—instead of a black dot, this one looked like it was on fire— and when it landed in the abandoned city of Charlestown, a house burst into flame. Soon all of Charlestown was on fire, and a great cloud of smoke rose up over the two armies.

XV. Mixed Emotions

Through the smoke, Ben and his friends watched as the red-coats marched toward the provincial soldiers. The British believed that the militiamen would run in panic when confronted with the impressive sight of 2,000 soldiers marching toward them. But they did not run.

Later the boys learned that Old Put told his men to hold their fire until they saw "the whites of the enemies' eyes." Only then,

when the British soldiers were an easier target, did the provincials fire. The boys cheered when most of the British soldiers fell down, but there were also tears in Ben's eyes. He remembered that winter day when a British officer had kindly fixed the boys' sledding run, and Ben didn't want that officer to die.

The British retreated, but General Howe ordered them to try again. So they marched up the hill a second time and were again cut down as they approached the provincials. Somehow, though, General Howe, whom they could see standing all alone near the provincial line, survived. Once again, Howe ordered his men to regroup at the bottom of the hill, where they were joined by hundreds more soldiers from Boston. It was time for one last try.

XVI. The Bitter End

Conquer or die!" was the cry of the British soldiers as they marched up the hill a third time. Once again, the provincials held their fire until the last possible second. But this time, the British were in narrow columns instead of a long, wide line, and even though many of them fell, those behind them kept coming up the hill. About this time, the provincials started to run out of gunpowder. Then they fought with rocks and the butts of their muskets. But they could no longer hold the British back, and Colonel Prescott was forced to order a retreat.

XVII. Not Defeated

Most of the provincial soldiers didn't stop running until they were back in Cambridge. But not Old Put. He joined Ben and his friends on Prospect Hill and ordered them to start digging a fort. If the British should follow them into Cambridge, a fort on Prospect Hill was the only hope of saving the provincial army. All night, Put and Ben and the other boys worked on their earthen wall. It was desperate and exhausting work, made all the more terrible by the thought of all those enemy soldiers streaming across Charlestown Neck. But the British never came.

The British soon built their own fort on the Charlestown peninsula, this time on Bunker Hill instead of Breed's Hill, where they could keep a careful eye on the provincials in Cambridge. The British had won, but even General Howe had to admit that the victory had come at too great a cost. Almost half his soldiers—close to a thousand men—had been killed or wounded. The provincials had turned out to be far better soldiers than the British had ever expected. And as more and more soldiers joined the patriot cause, conditions only got worse for the British in Boston.

XVIII. The New Commander

Two and a half weeks after the Battle of Bunker Hill, on July 2, General George Washington arrived to take over as commander of what was to be called the Continental Army. He was the opposite of Old Put. Instead of friendly, fat, and scruffy, Washington was tall, dignified, and perfectly dressed. Under Washington's calm and forceful leadership, the army would become more organized, like the British.

Four days after General Washington's arrival, on July 6, a ceremony was held atop Prospect Hill, where Ben and his friends had helped Old Put build his fort. Put had taken the mast from a ship and turned it into a flagpole. He gave a signal, and a big white flag with a green pine tree and the words "An Appeal to Heaven" was soon flying in the breeze. The soldiers gave three cheers while a cannon was fired from the rampart of the new fort.

For Ben, who was beginning to enjoy the life of a soldier, it was an exhilarating moment. He was proud to be a part of the fight for freedom.

XIX. Reunited

One afternoon, Ben went to Cambridge with several soldiers, to collect their weekly provisions. He was walking along the road with a basket of food in his arms when a horse-drawn carriage suddenly stopped beside him. The next thing Ben knew, a very thin and angry man was shaking him within an inch of his life. One of the soldiers stepped forward and said, "Don't shake that boy, sir, he is our clerk."

Only then did Ben realize that the thin and angry man was his father! After four months in British-occupied Boston with little food, his father had lost so much weight that Ben hadn't recognized him. The thought of his parents suffering in Boston while he had all the food he could eat in Cambridge made him feel sad, almost ashamed.

"Benjamin," his father said, "why didn't you put all those years with Master Carter to good use and write your mother a letter? She was worried to death!" When Ben had no reply, his father broke into an unexpected smile. "I think you boys were having too much fun to put pen to paper!"

Soon they were at Old Put's headquarters. The general agreed that Ben, who was only thirteen years old, must go with his father, and he granted the boy "an honorable discharge."

XX. The Apprentice

Ben and his father traveled forty miles to the town of Worcester, where their old neighbor and friend Isaiah Thomas had moved to resume publishing his newspaper, the *Massachusetts Spy*. Isaiah agreed to take Ben on as an apprentice. Ben had enjoyed his time in Old Put's regiment, but working as a newspaperman would prove to be the love of his life.

Isaiah's printing office was on the first floor. At night, Ben and another young apprentice slept in a small upstairs room called a garret. Since Isaiah Thomas couldn't afford to buy them a bed, the boys had no choice but to sleep on the rags that Isaiah collected for the papermaker. But compared to sleeping on the cold ground in a tent, it wasn't bad at all.

The *Massachusetts Spy* kept the people of New England informed about what was happening in Boston, and in March 1776 the newspaper announced that the British had finally left the city. Washington's army had built a fort on top of Dorchester Heights and mounted cannons that could have easily sunk the British warships and destroyed Boston. British general William Howe realized

he must abandon the city and resume the fighting somewhere else.
A few days later, Generals Howe and Washington agreed that if
the British left Boston without setting the buildings on fire, they
would be allowed to depart in peace.

On March 17, General Howe and his army of 9,000 soldiers, along with about 1,000 colonists who called themselves "loyalists" because they remained loyal to the British king, crowded into more than 150 ships. It was the biggest fleet anyone had ever seen in Boston Harbor.

XXI. Independence!

A few months later, in the middle of July 1776, word reached Worcester of the signing of the Declaration of Independence. Up until then, the war had been about preserving what the patriots called their "English liberties." Now they were fighting to create a new and united American nation.

On July 14, Benjamin Russell went with Isaiah Thomas to the South Church in Worcester. A huge crowd had assembled outside the building. In his hand, Isaiah held a copy of the Declaration of Independence, which had just arrived from the Continental Congress in Philadelphia. Ben watched as Isaiah stood on the porch of the church and began to read. "We hold these truths to be self-evident," he read in a loud voice, "that all men are created equal, that they are endowed by their Creator with certain unalienable rights, that among these are Life, Liberty and the pursuit of Happiness."

When he finished reading, the crowd burst into cheers. The Worcester militiamen fired their muskets. Everyone laughed and talked about how General Washington and his army would one day defeat General Howe, and America would become a great nation.

On the side of the Worcester Court House, there were the King's Arms—a brightly colored sign with the figures of the lion and the unicorn, representing England and Scotland. Ben and his friends climbed up a ladder, removed the wooden sign, and threw it in a large bonfire. It was all part of what Isaiah Thomas later described in the pages of the *Massachusetts Spy* as "a joyful celebration"—words that were set into type by the now fourteen-year-old Benjamin Russell.

Note from the Author

BENJAMIN RUSSELL (1761–1845) grew up to become one of the leading newspapermen of his day, ultimately serving as a representative in the Massachusetts state legislature. My account of Benjamin's experiences in and around Revolutionary Boston is based primarily on two sources: Francis Baylies's *Eulogy on the Honorable Benjamin Russell* (1845) and a biography of Benjamin Russell in *Specimens of Newspaper Literature* (1850) by Joseph Tinker Buckingham. In certain instances I have invented dialogue; I have also interwoven incidents from several other historical sources, including the letters of John Andrews (a Bostonian who relates the sledding episode) and William Gordon's history of the Revolution (in which he tells of the boy's comment to General Percy about the song "Yankee Doodle"). Whether or not these incidents involved Benjamin Russell (and they very well could have), they are known to have happened to boys just like him during the Revolution. For citations of these and other sources, see my *Bunker Hill: A City, a Siege, a Revolution*. Today, Isaiah Thomas's printing press can be seen at the American Antiquarian Society, an organization in Worcester, Massachusetts, that Isaiah Thomas founded in 1812.

—Nathaniel Philbrick

Note from the Artist

THE REVOLUTIONARY WAR ERA occurred long before the existence of photography. While researching this period, I had to rely on old drawings, paintings, maps, engravings, and illustrations. Not all are exactly accurate, but they had to serve as the source of inspiration for my depictions of Ben's world. I have made every effort to be as accurate as one can be using such sources. In addition, I also took photographs of a few models in costume. With this in mind, I have tried my best to visualize Ben's time and place of 1775–76 in Boston, Massachusetts.

—Wendell Minor

"Resistance to something was the law of New England nature."

—Henry Adams